Tonks' Wild Adventures

Dedicated to: Max, Gracie, and Dean. I'll love you forever.

First paperback edition September 2023
Book design by Samantha Harvey
ISBN (paperback)
ISBN (ebook)

Tonks sits by the window,
day by day.

She eats all of her treats,

and runs and plays.

There is one thing that Tonks does not like. No, she fills with anger just at the sight.

Tonks hisses and growls at the two cats outside. They have never crossed paths with her. She's not even willing to try.

Hello!

They talk and wave,
just trying to be friendly but,
the look that Tonks gives
the two is full of envy.

Today it's sunny,
so she runs out the door.

Tonks travels down the sidewalk, but she's curious for more.

With a blue sky above and warm air against her fur.

Tonks' day is going perfectly as she gets to the store.

The owner is happy to see her and brings out some treats. Tonks mews her thanks as she takes her food back out onto the street.

a mean skunk
called Lisa corners
her and growls,

"Give me your sweets, or i'll spray you and you'll stink for hours!"

Tonks runs to her left,
but gets stuck as Lisa prowls.

As the mean skunk gets closer,
it growls and scowls.

Tonks cries and says,
"Please, leave me be!"

But Lisa says, "No!"
because she is too mean.

She hides behind her paws,
waiting for Lisa to roar.

When Tonks opens her eyes,
she can't believe what she sees

The two neighbourhood cats come from behind the trees.

"Give us your friend, you mean ole' skunk!" Marley, the cat, shouts. Tonks is super grateful. She doesn't know what she was fussing about.

"Go away, you two!" Lisa stomps toward the others. Tonks cowers even lower, preparing to take cover.

Lisa's tail goes up,
causing Marley to jump

He lands near the others
with a big loud thump!

Castiel leaps in with a hiss and a swat.
Frustrated with Lisa, he says, "Say sorry! You know that you've been caught."

The **THUNDER** arrives, making things tricky.

Tonks jumps over the trashcan,
even though it was really stinky.

Lisa gets scared as
the rain starts dripping.

She yells,

"I'm sorry!"

and runs away tripping.

The clouds part, and the rain begins to clear. Castiel, Tonks, and Marley jump with cheer!

"Lets get you home." Marley pats Tonks back. She smiles and tosses them her extra snack.

When Tonks makes it safely back to her door, she praises her new friends and falls asleep right on the floor.

Now when Tonks lays in her window, day by day,

she waves and purrs
to her new friends all day.

Thank you for reading Tonks' Wild Adventures: These Cats Got Your Back!

Stay tuned to see what Tonks the Cat is up to in her next Wild Adventure.

www.ingramcontent.com/pod-product-compliance
Ingram Content Group UK Ltd.
Pitfield, Milton Keynes, MK11 3LW, UK
UKHW060116300726
14090UKWH00002B/229

* 9 7 8 1 7 3 8 8 5 6 0 3 9 *